Published by
Green Hope 2019

Published by arrangement with Green Hope publishers a division of Green Hope Youth Empowerment Initiative

Green Hope Youth Empowerment Initiative Reg CAC/IT/NO 51589

ISBN 978-978-972-820-6

Mind

I don't
Want to
Change your mind
I want
To know
Your mind

Such power
Transforms
Us both

Seeing

I choose to see you
As I look deeply into your eyes
I wish to see you for what you've
become
But not in the pennies and trinkets in
your pocket

I choose to see; your strength of
character
I choose to learn your soul
And preferably what you have done
with the talents therein
I choose to see beyond the superficial
Don't misunderstand me you look good
or not
I look through that
To the heart of the matter

I choose to see what motivates you
How you reason
And what you do when no one is
watching
How large your heart is
And how you feel in your smallest
moments
When I see you, I look beyond what I
see
To the heart of the matter
And then I see you

Arise

Arise to Self
Acceptance

Spurt

The seed cannot
Grow in the light
Respect your dark place

I thought this
Darkness was meant to
Destroy me

But I was being formed
Like a child in the womb
Like a seed in the soil

Needs

A new business
Is like a jealous lover
It needs
Obsessive attention

A new business
Is like a jealous lover
It needs
Obsessive attention

Words

You take everything to heart
You don't protect your heart
Don't beat yourself up
 it is counterproductive
Learn and move on
Don't let mistakes eat you up
Eat them up

No one person is experiencing life in the
same way
Don't compare your shortcomings,
mistakes, blessings, and successes
Be careful who you let in
You hardly ever are the same

You have one shot of making your life
an art
Mix all your colors and paint

There are some things only practice
would teach you
There are some things only inspiration
can lead you
Wisdom, skill, knowledge three
transforming components when joined
together
Happiness is a choice is not even a
feeling it is a state of mind
Work on your state of mind per second
This is your true task

Within

I kept looking

For something
Out of this world

But out of this world
Was beneath my nose
Beneath the stars
Within my heart

Sides

What is on the other side
Of
your
Perception

What is on the other side
Of
your
fear

What is on the other side
of
Your
Perspective

Hearts way

My heart
Lures me
To you

Even though
I've built
Strong Walls

I know my heart
Would let me
Through the window
Back to you

Resemblance

I heard that your
World
Is a
Resemblance of
Your
Heart

See way

They were misinformed
 By their circumstance
That there was
No way forward
But there's
Always a way
Forward

Acceptance

I am tired
Of trying
To prove
Anything

Accept my
Colors if you
Truly
Love me

Myself

I stepped out of Fear
And found me
By the door

Nature or Nurture

Nature or Nurture
You can become

Tough

Maturity
Is having a tough
Skin of positivity

Listen

I listen to people
Not what they say
But what they are
Not saying

Be quiet
I want to hear from you

Lifestream

Believe in
Your business
If not
Nobody else would

Trust- To rely on

You say you have Faith
Yet your soul dies
From anxiety

It falls from grace
For without faith
Our God can't be pleased

Even we can't be pleased
By people
Who have no faith in us
Talk more of our able God

Trust
And find peace
And faith in God

All

Everyone
Wants to
Be whole

Yet we are
All broken

Simplicity

Sometimes being simple is what you
need to be absolutely stunning

Soft Walk

A step at a time
And one day
You are everything
You need to be

Be patient and kind

Soft Walk

A step at a time
And one day
You are everything
You need to be

Be patient and kind

Individuality

If the sun
Was better
Than the moon
Why do we have night?

Just because
It shines
Brighter
Doesn't mean
The moon
Has lesser
Impact
On Humanity
And her universe

Customers

Customers are always right
That's a lie

But who cares
Just keep them happy
By making them feel
They're always right

So the money and referrals keep
Coming in

Eaten

You called me
Sweetheart
And ate
My heart
And of course
I died from
Naïve sweetness

So many things
You can be
But one thing
You have to be

Locate your Purpose
And be everything
You have to be

Peace

I make excuses
For people Just
To keep
My peace of mind

The Joke

The Joke
Is on you
Because you refuse
To laugh
At your failures
And get right up

The Joke

The Joke
Is on you
Because you refuse
To laugh
At your failures
And get right up

Take back

Whatever Pride
Has taken from you
Let Humility
Give back
To you

Forgiveness

Forgive Everyone
And
Forgive yourself

There's no liberty
To truly feel life and live life
With the burdens of offenses
And betrayals you carry
In your red heart born free
But now caged

I am

I am
not scared of winning
I am
not scared of losing
 I am
scared of not honestly living out
my individuality
Coloring the earth with crayons of
my soul

Become

Insist
On your
Becoming

Transform
To
Your Core

The world
Awaits to
Meet
You

Be Assured

Sometimes you give
Your best
And you wouldn't win
In the literal sense

Know that
God has blessed you
God cherishes
Your effort

Offense

You offended me
With your offense
But I didn't take offense
Because I didn't want
To be imprisoned
By your offense
And become
The offended

Life's Adventure

Your either living
Your adventure
Or you're
Killing the story of your life

Imperfect Perfect

Never wait
For your life
To be perfect

To have a
Perfect life

Never wait
For your life
To be perfect

To have a
Perfect life

Love Cry

She was all he wanted
And so he made his way
Right through her heart

Her soul remained
Untouched of him
You figure the ending

You don't walk
Into a humans soul
They invite you in

If love could be forced
Who could ever
Utter a broken heart

Unserious seriousness
I think
People have
Gotten too
Serious
About the unserious
Things of Life

Dice of Chance

I am not scared of taking chances
I am scared of chances taking me
By not taking chances

And so I take my chance
I strike chance first
This is the only way for more chances
Of winning chances

Start
Don't be scared of starting your life

Rebelling

I can write but I don't take my pen, I
rebel against my own words

Rebelling

I can write but I don't take my pen, I
rebel against my own words

Relax

You see
Most of
Our pain
Comes from taking things
Too personally

Live and Let Live

Sowing and Reaping

A wise farmer
Sows good seeds
A wise entrepreneur
Sows
Good value

R.E.S.T

Residual
Energy
Saved
Timely

Rise and Fall

Daring enough to fall
For you
But love was always supposed to be
A Rising

Love's Hurt

I wished the
Cupid told
You

The Arrow
Would hurt

Process

After the magic
Lies the
Magic
Of true love

Unbox

There is no box
There is you inside your perception or
outside
Your perception
Step outside your perception and
receive
Some fresh air

Faiths Fate

At what point
Does faith
Become Fate

Content

I dare you
Show me
Love without contentment

Content

I dare you
Show me
Love without contentment

Beautiful
Roses form too
They weren't born
This beautiful

What's the point?

At some point, there has to be a point

BUT MINE

I do not want to live anyone's life
But mine
Not at the border of people's
expectations
But at the heart of mine

Flexibility is a Goal
Conceptualize your life
And be flexible enough to know
Life is not static

Flexibility is a Goal
Conceptualize your life
And be flexible enough to know
Life is not static

Myself

I worked and walked
Back to myself
Not because
I wasn't fine where I was
But I needed to be awesome

Sassy

If my simplicity doesn't
Thrill you
Then let my complexity drill our Bond

If my simplicity doesn't
Thrill you
Then let my complexity drill our Bond

Pardon my objectivity

If we are all living fake lives
Then we are all masquerades
Parading as humans

Pardon my objectivity

If we are all living fake lives
Then we are all masquerades
Parading as humans

Problem-less Problem

Your problem is not your problem
But the way you handle it
Becomes your problem

Every one

I am sorry
 If you have failed
But so has every one

Wall puzzles

What if they were
No walls
It was just artwork and puzzle

Tell Me

Fear tells us
 Self-preservation
Over instincts
Instincts tell us
Self-preservation
Over fear

Soul Feeds

You gave

Your neighbour
Food to eat
But it was
Your soul that feed

Leverage

Leverage
Might always produce
More
Than hard work
Do not get me wrong
Hard work is very
Important
So don't waste it all

Leverage your hard work

Self-Competition
Have you ever found that you lost
hope?
But hope never left

Have you ever found that you lost love?
But love never left

Is it possible that it was never about
losing but living through?

If you've ever passed through
The fiery
Storm
You would know what I mean

It's not about losing or winning
It's about leaving and becoming

For every man must lose and win
But few ever become
You can lose and win unconsciously
But to become takes focus and never
giving up

Those who thought they were
competing with the world learned the
hard way

Show me your face

Show me your face
I am sure you can't tell which face is
yours
So many faces you project to the world
Even you have gotten lost in your
worlds
Each face
Each world of ignorance you dwell in

Let humility, love, hope, and faith be
your guide to your true face
You'll find peace and this piece of yours
will find you happiness
Contentment and posterity in
prosperity

Show me your face of love, honesty,
and tranquillity
Show me your true face

Character

Do not listen
To the temptation
 To act
 Out of character

Fragile

I am as fragile
As you are

I do not let my fragility
Steal my strength

Wake up

Wake up slumbering genius
From the slumber of mediocrity
For it is eating your soul away
I remember you
We met a time before
The passion that burst through your
soul
Conquering and consuming

Wake up slumbering genius
You are the light of the world
A city that cannot be hidden
Do not let your dying fire die
Pull down your dreams from the
heavens into the earth
Consciousness
Color your world with the beauty of
your uniqueness
Dare to believe again

Eureka
Life is
A constant motion

But a moment
 At a time
Break your life motions into great
moments of interactions

Between you and the universe

Eureka moments awaits us through
The little
Things that practically
Stare us
 In the face
There are always little moments that
inspire greatness
Our duty is to stay focused
And be alive to these crystallizing
moments

Know you

I know you

From where?

From my soul

One Butterfly

One butterfly left
From the butterflies I had
When we first met

Fiction
Our love is based on a true-life fiction

Granting
You took what I gave you for granted
So I took granted away
By turning the other way

Granting
You took what I gave you for granted
So I took granted away

Thrill

Let me come with you through your
lifetime
Thrill your life with me

The Other Way

Show me what love is for I have lost my
way
I met a lying lover that said the other
way

The Other Way

Show me what love is for I have lost my
way
I met a lying lover that said the other
way

Stared Lie

Then again she sat and stared deep into
my brown eyes and said I love you
But it had no impact on me
For I saw right through her
Her words meant nothing to her and
Nothing to me

Fearless

Fear less

Or

Fearless

You Can

Problems are meant to challenge you
Not consume you
Lift up yourself
And
Begin

I am not saying your fears are baseless
I am saying do not give them the bases
to stop you

I bet the stars preach a good message
But there's something about the
morning sky
That tells me, "go ahead you can do it'

On Arrival

The crowd would only cheer you up
when you have arrived
You need to cheer yourself up before
your arrival

Dead

A part of me would always Miss you
that part of me
 Is dead

A part of me would always Miss you
that part of me
 Is dead

Two

Is love the meeting of two bodies
Or the meeting of two souls

Think

Two burdens that kill
Humanity faster than death
Ego
And caring too much
Not of what is
But of what people think

Make It

Life is what you make of it
You are what you make of life

Make It

Life is what you make of it
You are what you make of life

Love

Love is love
And when you say, true love
You do not qualify love
You only disqualify
What isn't love

Love is love
And when you say, true love
You do not qualify love
You only disqualify
What isn't love

Enough

My love
Was not enough
Because of your love
Was not enough

Winning

Patience can cause you to win more
wars than going to wars with the intent
of winning

Dart

I wish you broke my heart
But you broke the dart

Identity

Yourself identify navigates your life

Regret

Stab regret in the back and step into
your future

Ignorance

I do not have a problem with
You
I have a problem with
Ignorance
Trying to drill a hole in your
Heart

Ignorance doesn't belong to
Anyone but it forces its way to
Stay true
Through our lack of knowledge
Or too much of it

How can we reduce the
The collateral damage of all of our
Individual ignorance

Well since it's individual
Ignorance's
It loses its collateral power

Pardon my ignorance

Roadmap

Your judgment of others
Gave us a road map
 To your soul

Your judgment of others
Gave us a road map
 To your soul

Motives

I thought I knew you
Until I found your motive
Hidden not too far from the
Corners of your heart

If you haven't known
The motive of a person
You sure do not
 Know that person

Soul Mate

Who is your
Soul mate?
The person who accepts your
Soul

Soul Check

Sometimes I just want to stare
In silence into my soul
It is called soul check

Sometimes I just want to stare
In silence into my soul
It is called soul check

Incomparable

When you compare yourself
 With others
You lose a part of your
Incomparable self

Do Not Fight

Do not fight the darkness
Bring in the light
Darkness doesn't fight
It either rules in or bows out

Faiths Power

Do not let go
Of your faith
Let your faith
Fill you with power

Aliens

If we are all seeing the world
From our worlds
Then earth is multidimensional
Aliens of the same world

Aliens

If we are all seeing the world
From our worlds
Then earth is multidimensional
Aliens of the same world

Smile

You made me smile
And others caught joy from
My happiness
How amazing how you touch
Many lives
Through one life

I AM

If I am what I think
The problem isn't me
The problem is in what I think

I AM

If I am what I think
The problem isn't me
The problem is in what I think

Present

As you present presents
Be also present in your life
And be also a present to those
Around you by being an
An epitome of love and hope

And also remember your life is
A present from God
And also remember the
Presents God has given you
And gives you each present day

And remember also you are a
Present to the world
If you would unwrap yourself
Presenting your gift to the
World

And God will receive praises
Because of your steps on earth

Be present and let love lead

Present in everything you do
Accept faith as your way
And hope as your light

Evolving

Maybe the reason why you are
 Broken
It's because it's time to break
Forth

Broken
Into
Wholeness

Quite

Be
Quite
I want to
Hear you

Be
Quite
I want to
Hear you

Faith Card

Faith is not putting all your
Cards on the table
Faith is putting the card as
Directed by God on the table

Faith isn't desperation
Faith is trust

Love you

Intimate me
 With your deepest
Stories
I want to crawl into your soul

Love you

Intimate me
 With your deepest
Stories
I want to crawl into your soul

Non-compliance

Plainly
I failed
To comply
With my doubts

Story

If you are not telling me the full story
Are you telling me a lie?

If you are telling me the full
Story
 Are you telling me the truth?

If we predominantly see the happenings
of life from our perception
Regardless of cultural or educational
background and emotional maturity
The truth might not win in all cases

But who is counting the wining truths
and the losing lies
If you are counting
 Why are you counting when you might
be biased?

Well for sanity sake let justice and
morality lead
And don't argue any further
There is hardly an absolute in the facts
of life
This is why it is life
Quality and quantity differs
And time doesn't make it any easier
If only time was still
Well this argument is for three other
days

Extra

Nothing makes an extraordinary man
But the person that goes the extra mile
It is the extra mile that brings out the
The extraordinary man in you

Faith

Faith doesn't move God
 Faith moves us
To get into the position of what God has
already done for us

Robot

Who is winning?
Man or technology
 I think the man is technology

Who is winning?
Man or technology
 I think the man is technology

Handcuff

Pride is not chain around your wrist
Like bracelet
Pride is handcuff

Humble

Humility beats pride at its own game
Not because pride isn't strong
But
Humility is not weak

Who are you

You are not the person
You see in the mirror
You are the person
You do not see
In the mirror

Mass Killing

Procrastination doesn't kill you
 It kills your dreams
Your killed dreams
 Kills your soul
Your killed soul
Kills your heart
Your killed heart
Means you died
At some point
In the Mass Killing

Perfect Lie

We have to paint a perfect picture
And so we paint a lie
But is there a perfect lie?

Train

If you feel stuck
You probably are not stuck
It is a feeling

If you are stuck
You probably are not stuck
I mean everything moves
Atomically

Hope

As progressives, we should be able to
get our minds off troubling thoughts
And go back to it refreshed
Making better decisions
On the way forward
And seeking quality advice when
needed
Hopelessness doesn't come from
hopeless situations
But from hopeless self-pity
And unproductive thoughts

Most problems lose steam from fresh
thinking

One

If you need to build
And you cannot
Spare you, neighbour
One block
You are building
A house of stone

Lust

Lose the world
If you must
But do not lose yourself

And Indeed
If you lose yourself
Get rid of all the lust
You were never lost

Unlearn

I question my thought
I bring my old way of reasoning
To my new way of thinking
Welcome I say

A greater learning skill
Is the ability
To unlearn

A step

Most times we need to take one step
From fear and faith would begin to
manifest
Other times one pattern change in the
way we think
Some times to see the big picture
We need to look away for a split second

I mean life-transforming changes can
come in the smallest of ways
This means it is possible to grow
 It is possible to transform
It is possible to evolve

Hate

Hate
 Are like holes
 They perforate
 Your goodness

Growing

Sometimes I try so hard to remember
Important information that is useful to
me
And so I jot it down
I forget the jotter

Wow is growth so hard
But here's what I do
I would take the effort to jot it down in
my heart
It's harder, harder than the paper jotter
But it's safer, safer in my heart
I take the effort so I can grow

See angle

I think a narrow perspective says
We shouldn't
See things from every perspective

And yet every perspective
Is the only way I am sure we aren't
blind

See angle

I think a narrow perspective says
We shouldn't
See things from every perspective

And yet every perspective
Is the only way I am sure we aren't
blind

Free Happiness

Society has programmed us
"You need to be happy for a reason"
But I beg you
Be happy for no reason

God's Trust

When you trust
God
Trust shows you its true meaning

Myself and I

I am
Always with myself
When I am with people

Myself and I

I am
Always with myself
When I am with people

Words

Too many words
It can't be heard

Silence isn't as golden
As good communication

Good communication
Isn't as costly as too many words
To die in silence is to die twice

Want

You want to change your perspective?
Change what you are saying to yourself
You want to change your life?
Try to see things differently
You want to grow?
Make a decision to grow
You want to stand out?
 Be yourself
You want to shine?
 Shine your skills

You want to be happy?
 Take things easy
You want true friends?
 Be a loyal person
You want to be wise?
 Learn and stay humble
You want to be knowledgeable?
 Read and stay alone sometimes
You want to learn to forgive?
Stop thinking about the hurt; Let it go
You want to understand yourself?
Listen to your heart, not your ego

Adaeze Charlyn Udom holds a BSc in Policy and Strategy from Covenant University. She is also a certified Educational Leader from Harvard University, Boston USA.
She has successfully founded and led a team for all Green Hope Youth Empowerment Initiative programs and projects a registered Non-governmental initiative in Nigeria.
Udom is also a journalist, writer, and best-selling author.
She also has a certification course on global cuisine. She is friendly, warm and very detailed. She is the CEO of Evri Healthy Foods Limited.